GO: *Mobilizing the Body of Christ*

by

Michael Eugene Wood

Graphic Design by Duane Thomas
Book Editing by Elaine Parrish

All Scripture quotations are taken from the King James Version.

If you would like to contact Michael Wood Ministries,
please visit: www.bromike.org

TEACH Services, Inc.
PUBLISHING
www.TEACHServices.com • (800) 367-1844

Copyright © 2016 Michael Eugene Wood

Copyright © 2016 TEACH Services, Inc.

ISBN-13: 978-1-4796-0673-3 (Paperback)
ISBN-13: 978-1-4796-0704-4 (Saddle Stitch)
ISBN-13: 978-1-4796-0674-0 (ePub)
ISBN-13: 978-1-4796-0675-7 (Mobi)

TEACH Services, Inc.
PUBLISHING
www.TEACHServices.com • (800) 367-1844

Preface

This book is dedicated to every person out there who feels they are far from God. It is also dedicated to everybody's son, daughter, father, mother, brother, sister, relative, and friend who has never given his or her life to Christ. Help is on the way!

*O God, be not far from me: O my God, make haste for my help. (**Psalm 71:12**)*

Our prayer is that God will use this book to inspire us all to GO more quickly to help those who feel far from God to make a decision to give their life to Christ by believing in Him as their Savior.

- *And Jesus came and spake unto them, saying, All power is given unto me in heaven and in earth.*

- *Go ye therefore, and teach all nations, baptizing them in the name of the Father, and of the Son, and of the Holy Ghost:*

- *Teaching them to observe all things whatsoever I have commanded you: and, lo, I am with you always, even unto the end of the world. Amen. (**Matt. 28:18–20**)*

Most Christians know what the Great Commission says, yet many are not mobilizing on these instructions from the Lord. The Lord told us to "GO." Some have interpreted

Jesus' command to "GO" as meaning that we should believe in our hearts for the lost to be saved while remaining safely within the church building. However, GOing requires getting mobilized. The word "mobilize" means "to make (something) movable or capable of movement." It also means preparing and organizing for active service. In most military campaigns, when the commanding officers are ready to move the troops, they *mobilize* them. My question to each believer born again in the Lord Jesus Christ is: "Are you moveable? Are you capable of movement?" My question to each pastor is: "Are the members of your church prepared and organized to GO at a moment's notice? Are they actively seeking the lost outside your church building?" God has laid it on my heart that I should remind His people to "GO."

Where Are We GOing?

Over the last couple of decades, many changes have taken place in America and many demoralizing laws have been passed in our justice system. The world we live in continues to bend more and more toward a sinful, fallen state. As we look forward to Christ's return, God reminds us that one day there will be a new heaven and a new earth.

> *And I saw a new heaven and a new earth: for the first heaven and the first earth were passed away; and there was no more sea. (**Rev. 21:1**)*

As Christians, we should continue to remind ourselves that this sinful world is not our home. We are just passing through. Our home is in heaven. We are only here for a season. From the day that Christ left to be seated at the right hand of the Father until He returns for His church, we are in the season of the harvest of souls for Jesus.

> *Then saith he unto his disciples, The harvest truly is plenteous, but the laborers are few. (**Matt. 9:37**)*

Why are there so few laborers? I believe it is because of the way some may have interpreted what the Lord meant by "GO." Many interpret the word "go" as meaning "reach." Think about it—I can reach someone by phone, but it doesn't mean I need to go where that person is. Many Christians who talk about reaching the lost believe that as long as they give financially to the cause of reaching people for Christ they have obeyed the command to "go." Yet, reaching the lost is not necessarily the same thing as going to the lost who are around you. Many Christians regularly attend church every week. In our churches, we spend our time with other believers, fellowshipping together in prayer and worship. Once we are done fellowshipping with fellow believers, do we ever go out to speak to people who are not believers? How much time do we dedicate to seeking the lost?

There are still many people who do not know Jesus. Notice that I did not say that there are many who have not *heard of* Jesus. In America, many have heard of Jesus, yet they still do not know Him. There is a difference. There are many who do not know what it feels like to accept Jesus Christ into their heart as their Lord and Savior. Are they in our church pews—within the four walls of our church? No, non-believers do not regularly attend church. They don't believe in doing that. Are we going where they are through our community outreach programs? How many unsaved people are coming to our community programs and giving their lives to Christ?

We have all heard the saying, "People don't care how much you know until they know how much you care." Is that a Bible Scripture or is it merely human experience? This concept inspires many church leaders to spend a lot of precious money, time, and resources on meeting the needs of our communities to open up opportunities for non-believers to receive the gospel of Christ. Then they show their congregations where they have spent money in the community.

What leads us to choose this route as our primary means for fulfilling the Great Commission? Is it because it is more comfortable for members of the churches to throw money at a problem than actually getting up and going out to witness? Is it the fear of rejection in compelling people to come to Christ? Or maybe it is that, when sinners are approached with the gospel and they have a need, they don't want to hear about Jesus' death, burial, and resurrection. They want someone to show them love by taking care of their needs first. Now, don't get me wrong—there is nothing wrong with meeting people's needs. Jesus said that we are to give to the poor and needy. Should this be the primary way we are to teach the gospel to all nations? Jesus said:

> *Go ye therefore, and teach all nations, baptizing them in the name of the Father, and of the Son, and of the Holy Ghost.* **(Matt. 28:19)**

Jesus directed us to "GO" where the people are and teach them. Where are we going with our outreach programs and methods? How many people are accepting Jesus into their heart through these programs? Are all the resources we put into these programs bringing people to make a decision for Christ? What are we accomplishing in the number of people coming to faith in comparison to the time, effort, and money spent trying to reach them? Are we now relegating our evangelism efforts to our local communities through need-focused community outreach programs? Is this how Jesus did it? Ask yourself: Where are we going?

Who Should GO?

Who are the laborers for the Lord's harvest, and what are they doing?

As a Christian, have you ever asked yourself, "When was the last time I verbally asked a person to give his or her life to Christ and the person received Him as Lord and Savior?"

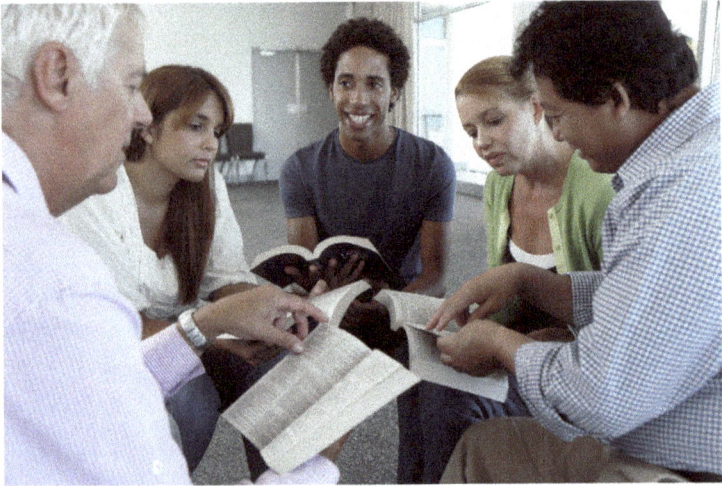

For many Christians, the answer is: Never. Why is that? Some people say that it is too personal to ask that question or they feel that it is not a popular thing to do if we want people to visit our churches. Some even depend on their pastor to ask the question from the pulpit because they believe that that is what the church is paying him to do. Do we think that only the pastor is called to "GO"? A pastor's calling is to lead and equip the flock to "GO."

Once you receive Jesus as your Lord and Savior, you find that, as a new Christian, your first calling is a call to prayer. This is because God wants a relationship with you. And if you love the Lord with all your heart and all your soul and all your mind and you put Him first, then you will hear the call to "GO."

There comes a certain stage of maturing in the Lord in every Christian's life that a person begins to reflect on what he or she has done in Jesus' name. Each person begins to hear the Holy Spirit from within asking, "Is this what you really should be doing for the Lord? Is this fruitful, or the best use of your time for Him?" We come to focus on how God can use us to lead people to Christ instead of becoming complacent and only doing things to get God to meet our needs. The love of God compels us to look outside of ourselves. Have we become inward-focused when it comes to efforts to reach people for Christ? Have we become like other non-Christian programs in training people to look to their community to meet their needs? Are we neglecting to compel people to come to Christ—to not accept "no" for an answer to our appeals?

Do you remember the day that you asked the Lord to come into your life? If you are like most born-again believers, you will say that that was one of the best days of your life. That was the turning point in your heart.

It was when you began to see things differently. In that moment of peace, all you could think about was knowing more about Christ, knowing Him in the power of His resurrection and fellowship of His suffering.

> *That I may know him, and the power of his resurrection, and the fellowship of his sufferings, being made conformable unto his death.* **(Phil. 3:10)**

Jesus was all that you wanted; He was all that you needed. You accepted Him as your Lord and Savior.

At the moment that many have received Jesus as Savior, they have sincerely and whole-heartedly believed that He redeemed them from the curse of sin and saved their souls from the destruction of hell. Yet, once they called Him "Lord," they did not fully surrender their spirit, soul, and body to His will. In other words, they kept a little reserve in their minds, holding back from His will that we all "GO."

This is the point at which many Christians may have unintentionally begun to focus inwardly about how to get God and their church to meet their spiritual needs. However, if you go back and remember what it was like to receive Christ for the first time, you will develop a hunger to "GO" and share what you experienced with others—that Jesus Christ is *your* Lord and Savior. Jesus said:

*Freely ye have received, freely give. (**Matt. 10:8**)*

I remember the first time I had the opportunity to walk a person through the gospel to receive Jesus as his Lord and Savior. We used to go out to our local neighborhood on the weekend and knock on doors to share Jesus. I recall being very nervous the first time I went out because I didn't know how people would react. I was also concerned about what I would say once I had a chance to talk to someone about the Lord. Yet, I had attended some training sessions on soul winning at my local church, which helped to prepare me to have questions to ask and answers to give in leading people to Christ. I asked the people whether they prayed and whether they attended church. I eventually asked them if they would like to receive Jesus as their Lord and Savior. Some people told me that they had already received Him in a saving relationship. Others told me that they were not ready to make that commitment. Some received Christ, praise God! Once I began doing this often, apart from the church group, it eventually became a way of life for me. Everyone has to start somewhere. If you start today by just making the decision to "GO"—I promise you—if you stay open to God, He will equip you with everything you need to fulfill your calling.

What Does It Cost to GO?

Within the mundane routines of church traditions, many of us have begun to focus inwardly without even realizing it. We have become self-centered. In some way, we have all been guilty of it. Sure, we say, "God use me! God use me!" and we begin the quest to find out what God wants us to do. We get busy serving in our local church. We serve the members, serve the needy, and we serve visitors to help keep our church fellowship adequately operating. All this is needed.

But as the years go by, in our daily service to God and our church, we may only get excited about souls being won for the Lord during certain events, such as Easter or Christmas or revival meetings. Why is that? Because normally these are the only times that there is a big push to win souls for Christ by inviting as many people to church as we can. Many who are non-members visit a church only on Easter and Christmas. On these occasions, the altars are full of people joining the Christian church, and the same routine begins all over again.

You may say, "Well, my pastor has an altar call every church service!" My question to you is: How many souls who are not already believers come to the altar and give their lives to Christ? Many times the altar is full of believers repenting for sin. We rightly rejoice in the repentance of believers and their rededication to the Lord. But how many of the people at the altar have never accepted the Lord before that day? Ask yourself: Are our altars full of repentant believers walking through the process of sanctification every week? Sure it looks great to our church members to think, *Wow, look at all those souls coming to the Lord!* Yet, God is saying:

Lift up your eyes, and look on the fields; for they are white already to harvest. (**John 4:35**)

The "fields" are not inside the four walls of the church. The fields are outside the church. I recently visited a megachurch that had about 2,000 people in attendance that day. After the sermon, the pastor asked people to stay seated, bow their heads, and raise a hand if they would like to give their life to Christ for the first time. He then began saying, "I see that hand. I see that hand. I see that hand." When he was done, a total of five hands were raised for actual salvation. He then led the people in the Sinner's Prayer, and the whole church rejoiced. That was awesome! Five souls came into the kingdom of God that day.

But how many more souls would we rejoice over if every Christian left the comfort of the church pews and went into the highways and byways "compelling people to come" to Christ every week?

> *And the lord said unto the servant, Go out into the highways and hedges, and compel them to come in, that my house may be filled. (**Luke 14:23**)*

What if you, as a Christian, began believing that you would personally win a soul a day for God? In seven days you would win seven souls for Christ. What if you came to worship service with a testimony of having led seven souls into the kingdom that week? That would be two souls more than a whole megachurch of 2,000 members was able to win in a week. What if every Christian began believing this?

This is not a comparison for the sake of competition. This is a comparison for accountability and stewardship of the resources and time that God has given His people. Child of God, Man of God, here is what I believe the Lord is asking us: Are we really getting the best bang for the donation buck that God is putting in our hands as stewards in winning souls for Him? For example, let's say that same church of 2,000 members, which had five new believers that day, received $200 from each member in tithes that week. That would be $400,000 that week. So in this example, it cost the church $80,000 for each soul it brought into the kingdom of God that week. (400,000 divided by 5 equals 80,000.) Are we getting the best bang for our donation buck? Are we being good stewards of God's money? This in no way reflects the spiritual efforts of every church, but there is a need of commitment for better stewardship and restructuring of our priorities to support the call of the Great Commission to "GO." Every church and every believer need to re-evaluate where they are putting their resources—their time, money, and effort—and ask the Lord whether we are using those resources to maximize the number of unsaved people accepting Jesus Christ as their Lord and Savior. First and foremost, every church should keep this primary purpose in mind: winning souls into the Kingdom of God.

How Do I GO?

Now compare the thought of compelling people to come to church to compelling them to come to Christ. All pastors, church members, and church leaders need to ask themselves this question: *Am I compelling people to come to a building or am I compelling people to come to Christ?*

How many people do you walk by in a two-foot vicinity in a single day? I judged this for myself and discovered that I came into contact with approximately 28 people that I could have spoken to about the Lord. That was 28 souls I could have asked the Lord to give me the courage to compel to give their life to Him. What if, out of those 28 people, ten actually spoke to me, five shared their life with me, and one gave their life to Christ that day? If I did this every day, that would be seven souls in a week. Now compare this to a megachurch that spends $400,000 on five souls a week.

"Well," some may say, "I need them to come to church before I can tell them about Christ." That's like asking, "Which came first, the chicken or the egg?" Do we need a building to win souls for Christ? Do we need a choir, a pulpit, or clean facilities to compel them to come to Christ? These things are really "nice to have" so that believers can have a place to come together and fellowship. Really, there is nothing wrong with these things. Yet, when we let these things hinder our focus on our call to

"GO," we are wasting time and money. Is this call really about our church, our fellowship, our needs, our vision, and our goals? Every goal for every church and every born-again believer should be aligned with the head of the Church, Jesus Christ. He didn't tell us to stay; He told us to "GO."

Sometimes I hear the excuse for not GOing: "The Lord tells us that some water and some plant and that He will provide the increase. So I am watering people with an encouraging word when I see them, and God will win them over when He's ready." Since this thinking is based on 1 Corinthians 3:6, let's read that Scriptural passage in context.

> 1. *And I, brethren, could not speak unto you as unto spiritual, but as unto carnal, even as unto babes in Christ.*

2. *I have fed you with milk, and not with meat: for hitherto ye were not able to bear it, neither yet now are ye able.*

3. *For ye are yet carnal: for whereas there is among you envying, and strife, and divisions, are ye not carnal, and walk as men?*

4. *For while one saith, I am of Paul; and another, I am of Apollos; are ye not carnal?*

5. *Who then is Paul, and who is Apollos, but ministers by whom ye believed, even as the Lord gave to every man?*

6. *I have planted, Apollos watered; but God gave the increase.*

7. *So then neither is he that planteth any thing, neither he that watereth; but God that giveth the increase.*

8. *Now he that planteth and he that watereth are one: and every man shall receive his own reward according to his own labor.*

9. *For we are laborers together with God: ye are God's husbandry, ye are God's building. (**1 Cor. 3:1–9**)*

Notice that these Scriptures are speaking from a pastoral role in raising up believers who are already saved. When you look closely, you will see that they are talking about Paul and Apollos preaching to believers at their church. These Scriptures are not about evangelism. They are about the spiritual growth of believers. Paul is talking about believers increasing in their spiritual maturity, not about adding newly born-again people to the church. Paul is saying they should be further along than they already are. They are in strife over whom they consider they were raised to follow. Some say it was Paul, and some say Apollos. Paul corrects them by saying they are disciples of both. Paul "planted" the church, and Apollos "watered" by helping to teach and disciple the church, but it was God who provided the increase in their spiritual growth. These Scriptures are about discipleship, or teaching how to follow Jesus, not about winning souls. "Watering" in this context is teaching and raising up a believer, not talking to a sinner for the first time. So the excuse, "I am watering the lost," is not in alignment with what Paul is saying in these Scriptures. We are to GO and win the lost, not water the lost.

There are some basic, practical things you can do to obey the commandment to GO.

- We need to GO after being trained on what it means to be a witness.

First things first: we must understand what it means to be a witness.

*But ye shall receive power, after that the Holy Ghost is come upon you: and <u>ye shall be witnesses</u> unto me both in Jerusalem, and in all Judaea, and in Samaria, and unto the uttermost part of the earth. (**Acts 1:8**)*

To be a witness is not to deliver an evangelistic message with Scriptures. It does not mean to preach to someone. To witness means to give your personal testimony. It means to get on the witness stand and tell people what Jesus has done in your life. Jesus sent His disciples as eyewitnesses for Him. You testify by giving your personal experience of the reality of God in your life.

• We need to GO after being equipped in the power of the Spirit. We need help to GO. Jesus sent the Holy Spirit as our helper. We can't do it alone.

*And I will pray the Father, and he shall give you another Comforter, that he may abide with you for ever. (**John 14:16**)*

• The Holy Spirit was sent to be our Comforter and Help, and when we GO in the power of the Spirit, He will help us win souls for Christ. The Holy Spirit is the One who touches and shines the light in a person's heart to help them receive Christ.

- We need to GO believing in faith.

- We need God to direct us to be at the right place and time to win a person's life over to Him. Putting our trust in God as we GO is key to believing He will work through us. We cannot GO by our own efforts. This may be the reason many have not been successful in winning souls. We need to be in faith, trusting God for hearts and minds to be open to listen to the gospel of Jesus Christ.

But let him ask in faith, nothing wavering. For he that wavereth is like a wave of the sea driven with the wind and tossed. (James 1:6)

- We need to trust God for the results. Because He told us to GO, we need to trust Him for the outcome for that given moment.

Finally, we are all called to be witnesses for the Lord! It is time for us, the Body of Christ, to rise up and GO out to the hurting and the lost. They may never come to visit our church and sit in our church pews. We need to be mobile in our outreach efforts by witnessing to people everywhere we GO in our daily lives.

We invite you to view the complete
selection of titles we publish at:
www.TEACHServices.com

scan with your mobile
device to go directly
to our website

Please write or email us your praises, reactions, or
thoughts about this or any other book we publish at:

TEACH Services, Inc.
P U B L I S H I N G
www.TEACHServices.com ● (800) 367-1844

Info@TEACHServices.com

TEACH Services, Inc., titles may be purchased in bulk
for educational, business, fund-raising, or sales
promotional use. For information, please e-mail:

BulkSales@TEACHServices.com

Finally if you are interested in seeing
your own book in print, please contact us at

publishing@TEACHServices.com

We would be happy to review your manuscript for free.